Published by Creative Education
123 South Broad Street, Mankato, Minnesota 56001
Creative Education is an imprint of The Creative Company

Art direction by Rita Marshall
Production design by The Design Lab

Library of Congress Cataloging-in-Publication Data

Hidalgo, Maria.
Light / by Maria Hidalgo.
p. cm. — (Let's investigate)
Summary: Discusses the nature and sources of light,
as well as its importance in our world.
ISBN 1-58341-230-1
1. Light—Juvenile literature. [1. Light.]
I. Title. II. Series.
QC360 .H53   2002
535—dc21   2001047890

First edition

2 4 6 8 9 7 5 3 1

LIGHT

MARIA HIDALGO

Creative Education

LIGHT
POWER

Solar power cells transform light energy into electrical energy. Solar energy is used to warm buildings and water, power machinery, and operate most space satellites.

Light carries life to Earth in the form of energy, radiation, and warmth. It creates intense weather extremes and triggers important events in the food cycle. While we see just one part of light's electromagnetic spectrum, light's invisible benefits sustain every form of life on the planet.

Right, solar panels
Far right, sunlit clouds

L I G H T
COLORS

In fall, as sunlight grows scarce, trees make less chloro-phyll, a green pig-ment necessary for growth. This makes other pigments, which reflect yellow and orange light waves, more visible.

Light is one of many ways that energy can travel. Moving through space, air, water, or other materials in waves, light is visible to the human eye as it is **emitted** or as it is reflected off surfaces. In other words, if light were not bouncing off this page into your eyes right now, the page would not be visible.

Above, autumn leaves
Right, the reflection of light off objects makes sight possible

As a form of **radiant energy**, light can become heat, and heat can become light. While only a fraction of the sun's energy reaches Earth's **atmosphere** and surface, light waves are still powerful enough to transfer energy to electrons in the air, land, and water, and generate heat.

Night goggles intensify reflected light waves that are too weak or outside of our visible light spectrum. A camera captures the waves and displays them on a screen.

7

LIGHT
F A C T

Dogs have a special reflective layer in their eyes that helps them see at night by sending weak light waves through the retina twice.

LIGHT
S P E E D

The speed of light traveling through empty space (a vacuum) is 186,282 miles (299,914 km) per second.

The sun's infrared and ultraviolet light are invisible to the naked eye

THE LIGHT SPECTRUM

The human eye sees only a small portion of the radiation that the sun delivers. Light delivers a wide range of electromagnetic radiation, including visible light, infrared light, and ultraviolet radiation. This full collection of wavelengths is called the electromagnetic spectrum.

Reflected green light waves give most tree and plant leaves their green color; other light wave colors, such as blue and orange, are absorbed.

Above, a tree reflecting green light waves
Left, a rainbow contains Newton's seven main color wavelengths

The visible light that arrives on Earth from the sun appears white, but it actually contains every color light wave and can be broken down into individual colors. One of the first scientists to investigate the different colors present in light was Sir Isaac Newton, an English scientist working in the late 1600s and early 1700s. He chose seven color names to identify different wavelengths: red, orange, yellow, green, blue, indigo, and violet.

L I G H T

ATTRACTION

Although moths are attracted to light in general, they don't seem to be fond of longer-wavelength yellow light, which is why people often install yellow-colored porch lights.

A prism refracting "white" light into separate wavelengths

Each color has its own wavelength. Red has the longest distance between waves (the lowest frequency), and violet has the shortest distance between waves (the highest frequency). Prisms break "white" light into its different wavelengths. Made of glass or another transparent material, prisms are precisely cut with perfect edges, **angles**, and flat surfaces that "bend" each incoming wave in a slightly different direction. This bending is called refraction. The light waves that emerge from the other side of the prism are organized by wavelength, with red light waves bent the least and violet bent the most.

ature has its own prism—water—and this prism is responsible for rainbows. When the sun's white light enters a raindrop, it refracts into different wavelengths. These light waves then reflect off the back surface of the raindrop, where they refract again as they pass out of the water. The reflection off the back of the raindrop sends the light waves out at the same angle as millions of other raindrops in the area, directing them out in a circular pattern. The result creates the curve in rainbows.

Remember the order of the colors in the visible spectrum, from longest wavelength to shortest, with the name Roy G. Biv: red, orange, yellow, green, blue, indigo, and violet.

A colorful garden reflected off the back surfaces of raindrops

LIGHT

*When the sun is directly above the **equator**, its light reaches the whole globe evenly, and night and day are exactly the same length. This is called an equinox.*

12

LIGHT AND THE SUN

Earth spins on a slightly tilted **axis** as it **orbits** around the sun at a distance of about 93 million miles (150 million km). This double circular motion, caused by the huge gravitational force of the sun, creates night and day on Earth, as well as the four seasons and the phases of the moon.

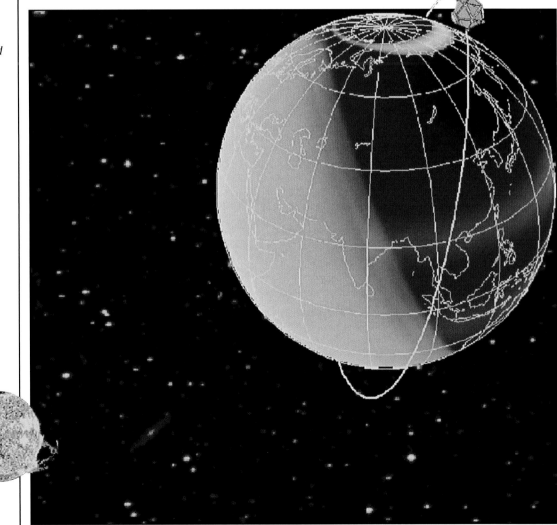

The sun, Earth, and Earth's orbiting moon

At any time as Earth turns on its axis, one half of the globe is in the full light of the sun, while the other half is in the dark. The side facing the sun and absorbing the light is experiencing its daytime hours. As the day progresses, the globe turns, and the day side turns away from the sun and experiences night. The energy transferred from the sun during the day is the foundation for Earth's food cycle, water cycle, weather, and life itself. Without the sun's light, Earth would be nothing but a cold, lifeless rock floating through space.

LIGHT
RETARDANT

Researchers have slowed the speed of light to 38 miles (61 km) per hour by shooting a beam of light through a cluster of sodium atoms.

LIGHT
SOURCE

The sun is only an average-sized star in terms of the Milky Way galaxy, but it is the biggest celestial body and the central anchor in Earth's solar system.

Top, the sun shining through the atmosphere Below, the moon reflecting the sun's light

LIGHT
INTENSITY

Twice a year, the sun reaches a position where it is as close to the North or South Pole as it will get. This date is called the summer or winter solstice.

For six months, Earth's **North Pole** tilts toward the sun. Because of this, the light waves from the sun don't have to travel as far to reach Earth's surface in the **Northern Hemisphere**. This tilt causes longer daylight hours. It also changes the angle at which light waves hit Earth, generating more heat for warm spring weather and hot summer days. During the other six months of the year, the opposite happens: the **South Pole** leans toward the sun, bringing summer to the **Southern Hemisphere** and winter to the Northern Hemisphere.

Summer at the South Pole brings melting ice and the return of penguins to their breeding sites

A light year is the distance that light can travel through empty space (a vacuum) in one Earth year. It's calculated to be about 5.88 trillion miles (9.46 trillion km).

The tilt of Earth's axis also causes at least one full day (24 hours) of sunlight at the North Pole during summer, **simultaneously** causing at least one full day of complete darkness at the South Pole. Arctic regions such as northern Norway experience a unique five-month summer. From mid-May to late July, the sun never sets over the very northernmost parts of these regions. This is called the midnight sun. During December and January, these same regions are plunged into darkness, as the sun never rises over the horizon.

The midnight sun shining above the North Pole

LIGHT
SATELLITE

The moon is about one-third the size of Earth and is believed to have originated when a large impact broke matter free from our planet.

LIGHT
BLOCK

When the moon's orbit positions it between the sun and Earth, preventing the sun's light from reaching Earth, a solar eclipse occurs.

A time-lapse photograph showing the moon's different phases

LIGHT AND THE MOON

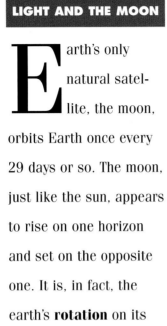

Earth's only natural satellite, the moon, orbits Earth once every 29 days or so. The moon, just like the sun, appears to rise on one horizon and set on the opposite one. It is, in fact, the earth's **rotation** on its axis that causes the illusion of their motion across the sky.

L I G H T
DISPLAY

Caused by intense solar activity exciting atoms in the upper atmosphere, the luminous aurora borealis can often be spotted on clear nights in northern parts of the world.

Above, the aurora borealis
Right, the moon

The moon does not have an energy source to create its own light; it merely reflects the sun's light. Earth casts a shadow across the moon, creating the different moon phases. When Earth completely blocks all of the sun's light, the moon is not visible and is called a "new moon." A "waxing" moon occurs when Earth's position allows the sun's light to reveal the first quarter of the moon after the new moon. A "waning" moon comes after the full moon, when Earth begins to block the sunlight again.

LIGHT AND WEATHER

The sun's light warms Earth's land, air, and water, transmitting energy in the form of electromagnetic radiation. An important process called "transfer of energy" occurs every time light delivers heat to a surface. The total amount of energy is always the same, but the energy can change from one form, such as radiant energy (light), to another, such as thermal energy (heat).

LIGHT
BEAM

A laser is an intense beam of light. The wavelength of a single color is amplified to release powerful and precise energy.

LIGHT
TERM

The word "laser" is an acronym (a word formed from the first letters of a name) for "light amplification by stimulated emission of radiation."

The sun is the source of all heat on Earth

LIGHT
ENERGY

The energy in an average lightning flash could light a 100-watt light bulb for three months. Unfortunately, there is no way to capture this energy because lightning is so unpredictable.

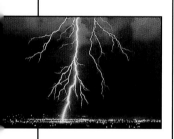

Above, lightning
Right, a tropical storm on Earth's surface as seen from space

Temperatures between two **adjoining** surfaces always seek **equilibrium**, meaning they want to be the same temperature. So as Earth's land heats up during the day, it transfers the warmth to the air above it. Warm air is less dense than cooler air, so the warm air rises, allowing cooler air to flow in below it. This motion creates wind and, in time, allows rain and other storms to circulate around Earth's surface.

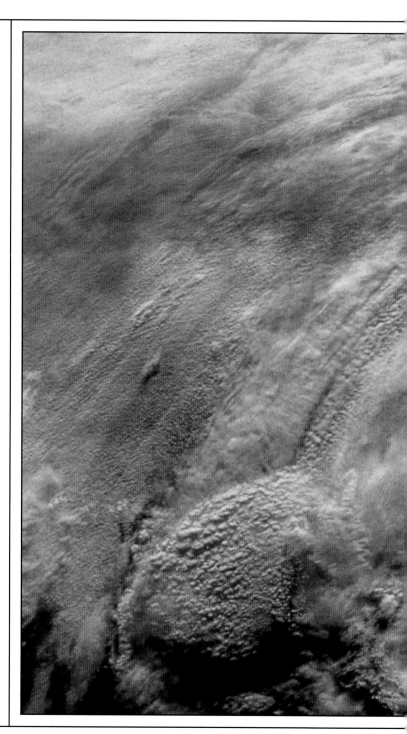

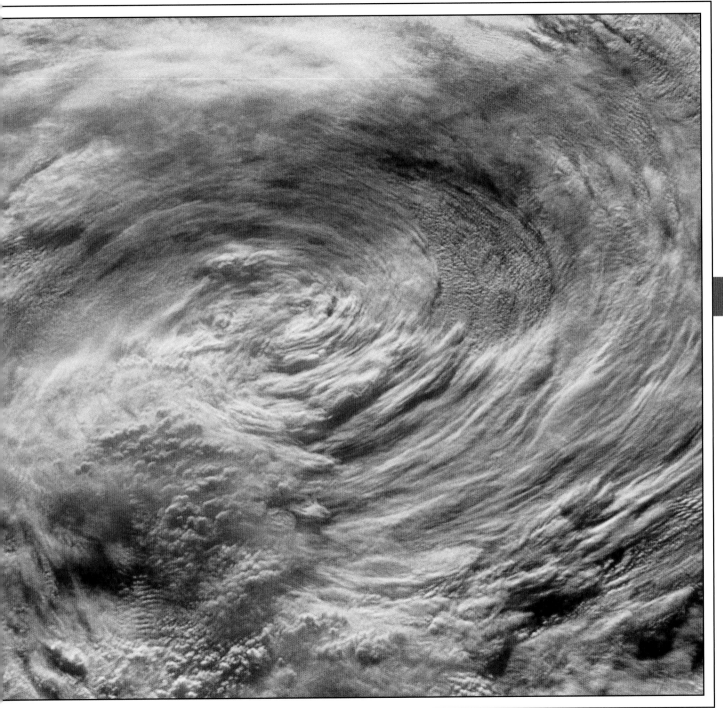

LIGHT
COLORS

The sky and the ocean appear blue because water molecules in the air and ocean scatter blue light waves easier than the waves of other colors.

unlight has a similar effect on Earth's oceans. Large bodies of water are able to hold vast quantities of heat, so they act as energy reservoirs. Like air, water that has been warmed rises and spreads out above cooler water, causing ocean currents. The sun's light also causes water to evaporate from the ocean surface, starting Earth's water cycle. Water evaporates, rises into the air, forms clouds, and returns to Earth as precipitation (rain, snow, or other variations). This moisture soaks into the ground, or collects in lakes and rivers, and eventually returns to the ocean to begin the cycle again.

Right, sunlight's heat triggers the earth's water cycle
Far right, water returning to Earth as rain

L I G H T

Cameras work much like the human eye, only instead of light waves hitting rods and cones, they hit a strip of light-sensitive film.

Above, a camera
Right, a brightly lit
ferris wheel in motion

LIGHT AND VISION

As light waves bounce off objects, they reflect into the human eye, causing the sense of vision to activate. While light carries both visible and invisible waves, the human eye responds only to the visible light waves.

The human eye is a slightly oval sphere with a clear front that allows light waves to enter. Light rays travel through the eye's lens and land on an inside lining called the retina. The retina is made of nerve tissue filled with millions of light receptors called rods and cones. These receptors interpret the light waves, create an image, and deliver it to the brain through the optic nerve.

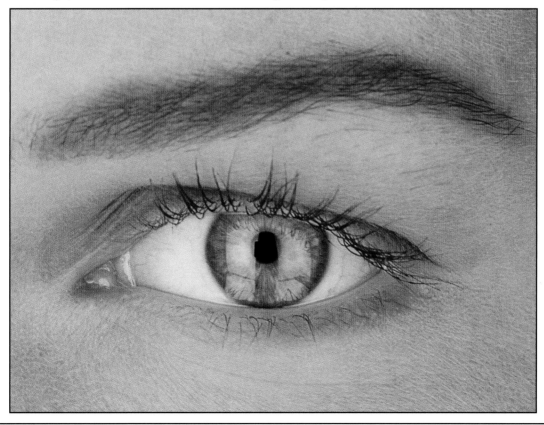

LIGHT
DANGER

Although invisible to the human eye, ultraviolet light from the sun can damage unprotected skin and cause sunburn, even on cloudy days.

LIGHT
PROTECTION

Sunscreen and sun block lotions help protect skin by reflecting invisible UVA rays and the more dangerous UVB rays.

The colored part of the human eye is a muscle called the iris

L I G H T
F A C T

When light waves enter the eye and form an image, the image is upside-down; the brain then has to flip the image over.

L I G H T
B U L B

An incandescent light bulb uses an electrical current to heat a fine wire called a filament until it glows and produces light.

Before electricity, candles were one of the only sources of light once the sun set

For an eye to see an object, light must somehow travel from that object and enter the eye. The light can be transmitted from the object itself (such as the sun, a light bulb, or a candle), or it can be scattered or reflected off the object (such as a mirror, this book, or any object that does not create its own source of light).

L ight waves reflect not just off shiny or glass surfaces, but off any object. Reflection occurs when a light wave hits a surface and then bounces back, just as a ball would, in a different direction. If there are no light waves to bounce off a surface (such as in a room with no windows and no artificial sources of light), vision is not possible. In fact, light is the only thing human eyes really see. Objects themselves do not have colors; they reflect certain wavelengths that the human eye perceives as yellow, red, purple, or any of a number of other colors.

LIGHT
IDENTIFICATION

Some insects can see ultraviolet light, helping them discern differences between flowers and other insects that otherwise look the same under visible light.

LIGHT
BIOLOGY

Fireflies are beetles that have light-producing chemicals in the tips of their abdomens. Frogs have been known to eat so many that they themselves glow.

Reflected light waves give all things color

LIGHT
ENERGY

Millions of years ago, green plants and plant eaters multiplied faster than they could be consumed. They eventually fossilized and became the fuels that power today's cars and create electricity.

LIGHT AND LIFE

The sun's radiation is the source for all biological energy on the planet, with light energy turning into chemical energy in a process called photosynthesis. This is the very start of all life on Earth. Plants capture the sun's light with their leaves and use the energy contained within that light to turn carbon dioxide, water, and minerals absorbed from the ground into oxygen and food. The oxygen is released into the air, while the food, in the form of sugars known as carbohydrates, fuels the growth of the plant.

Plant life converting the sun's energy to growth

LIGHT
COMMUNICATION

Light is used to communicate information through fiber optic cables, usually using thin glass strands and ultraviolet light.

LIGHT
MEDICINE

X-rays, with their extremely short wavelengths, can flow through bodies and are used to take internal pictures, where bones and other body parts cast shadows onto special film.

Rays of sunlight encourage plant growth and, in turn, feed hungry livestock

Without the sun's light, the food chain on Earth would not exist. Plants, fueled by the sun's energy, are eaten by herbivores (organisms that eat only plants), which, in turn, are eaten by carnivores (meat-eaters). Even the end of a plant's life supports other organisms. Decaying plants feed insects called decomposers that break the plant down into its most basic elements. The resulting nutrients enrich the soil and support the growth of new plants.

LIGHT

COOKING

Microwaves are low-energy light waves. Microwave ovens cook food by converting the light energy contained in these waves into concentrated heat energy.

30

LIGHT

TRANSPORTATION

Cars powered by solar energy don't contribute to air pollution and are three to four times more efficient than vehicles with gasoline engines.

Without light, life on Earth would not exist

It's easy to take for granted all that light does for us. We usually don't give it much thought—until it isn't there. Light enables us to see. It warms us. It cooks our meals. It changes our seasons and affects our weather. Light helps plants provide the food and oxygen upon which all life on Earth depends. And scientists continue to find new ways to manipulate and use light every day. One thing is clear: the power of light is the most important power on Earth.

Glossary

Two items are **adjoining** if they are touching or right next to each other.

Angles are created when two lines or planes intersect to form a corner.

The **atmosphere** is the thick mass of air that surrounds Earth; it's held in place by gravity.

Earth's **axis** is the imaginary straight line through the center of Earth around which the planet rotates.

Light is **emitted** when it is created and released by an object.

Earth's **equator** is the imaginary line that divides the globe in half around its center.

Equilibrium is a state of balance, where opposing forces are equal.

The **North Pole** is the northernmost point on Earth and marks the northern tip of Earth's axis.

The **Northern Hemisphere** is the half of Earth that lies north of the equator.

When a planet **orbits** a star, it travels on a circular path around the star.

Radiant energy is energy that travels as electromagnetic waves, including infrared light, visible light, ultraviolet light, x-rays, and gamma rays.

Rotation is a circular motion that returns an object to its original position.

If two things happen **simultaneously**, they happen at exactly the same time.

The **South Pole** is the southernmost point on Earth and marks the southern tip of Earth's axis.

The **Southern Hemisphere** is the half of Earth that lies south of the equator.

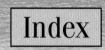

Index

Photographs by Corbis (Galen Rowell), Dennis Frates, The Image Finders (Jim Baron, Mark E. Gibson, Michael Phillip Manheim, Scott Pease), KAC Productions (Kathy Adams Clark, Greg Lasley), Tom Pantages, Science Photo Library (Oscar Burriel, NASA, John Sanford), Tom Stack & Associates (J. Lotter, Doug Sokell, Mark Allen Stack, Tom Stack, Spencer Swanger, Greg Vaughn, William L. Wantland, David & Tess Young), Unicorn (Richard Gilbert, Scott Liles, Dave Lyons, Dennis Thompson, Julie Walker)